I0006263

The Ultimate Guide to Making Money Online: Proven Strategies and Tips for Success

Jim Stephens

Published by RWG Publishing, 2023.

THE ULTIMATE GUIDE TO MAKING MONEY ONLINE: PROVEN STRATEGIES AND TIPS FOR SUCCESS

First edition. January 27, 2023.

Written by Jim Stephens.

Also by Jim Stephens

Kindle Publishing Made Easy: Autopilot Cash With Amazon Kindle!
Million-Dollar Secrets of the Amazon Associates: How They Make Money From the Biggest Online Shopping Mall
Self-Publishing Made Easy: The Easy Way to Self-publish Your Own Books!
Scam Busters: How to Avoid the Most Popular Scams of Today!
Affiliate Marketing and Blogging
The Quick and Easy Guide of Diamonds
Government Information
Hiking and Camping
Koi Pond
Law Information Guide
Motor Homes Research
Affiliate Marketing and Success Systems
Online Shopping
Outsourcing Ebooks and Software Jobs
Personal Loans
Private Jet Charters
Private Yacht Charters
Internet Marketer Alpha Dog
Networking and Social Dominance in the Twenty-First Century
Copywriting Best Kept Secrets: A Training Course for Writing Great Copy
Starting Your Home Business

Affiliate Marketing for Beginners: You Will Never Succeed Unless You Take The Opportunity

A Guide to Creating the Most Appropriate Budgets for You: Additional Cash in Your Pocket

Various Advantages of Membership Websites: With Membership Websites, Create a Passive Income

Affiliate Marketing Made Simple: Avoid Common Errors and Thrive in Successes

Article Marketing Made Simple: It Is Not Necessarily Difficult to Succeed

Blogging Made Simple: Blogging Can Be Lucrative

Advertising That Pays: Increase Your Traffic and Leads

The Complete Guide to Copywriting: Creating Words That Sell

Affiliate Marketing Made Simple

The Affiliate Marketer's Manual

Aquarium Maintenance Made Simple

Beginner's Guide to Online Video Marketing

Blogging Fundamentals: Blogging is the Next Big Thing

Techniques for Advanced Search Engine Optimization: On Autopilot, Increase Your Traffic and Profits!

Article Marketing Secrets

Beginner's Guide to Black Hat SEO

Super Guide to Snowmobiling: The Best Places to Have a Great Time

Forest Adventure With Friends: A Captivating Story With a Lot of Fun

How to Advertise Like a Pro

My Journey Through Life: A Personal Memoir

The Art of Crafting Short Stories: A Guide to Writing and Publishing

The Ultimate Guide to Making Money Online: Proven Strategies and Tips for Success

Battlefield of Honor: Bravery and Sacrifice Tested In Ultimate Battle

Echoes of the Past: Unveiling History's Secrets

Warrior's Code: The Unbreakable Ethics of a Warrior

AI-Powered Marketing: The Future of Digital Advertising

Beyond Words: How ChatGPT is Revolutionizing Communication
The Language of AI: Exploring the Power of ChatGPT
Talking to Machines: The Fascinating Story of ChatGPT and AI
Language Models
Uncovering the Unknown: Tales of Mysterious Discoveries
Shadow Squadron: Inside Covert Operations
The Last Stand: The Triumph of Bravery in Desperate Times
Valor in the Skies: Courage and Sacrifice in Aerial Warfare
Courage, Sacrifice, and Honor: Tales from the Frontline Heroes

Table of Contents

Introduction: Setting Your Goals and Mindset for Success

———

M aking money online is a great way to achieve financial freedom and create a lifestyle of your choosing. However, as with any venture, it requires a clear plan, a positive attitude, and a willingness to put in the work to achieve your goals. In this chapter, we will discuss how to set your goals, understand your motivations, and develop a mindset that will set you up for success in your online earning journey.

Setting Your Goals

Before you start your online earning journey, it's important to set clear and measurable goals. This will help you stay focused and motivated as you work towards your financial objectives. When setting your goals, consider the following:

- What do you want to achieve financially? How much money do you want to make?
- What are your short-term and long-term goals?
- How will you measure your progress?
- What resources do you need to achieve your goals?
- What are the potential obstacles or challenges you might face, and how will you overcome them?

Once you have a clear understanding of your goals, you can create a plan of action to achieve them.

Understanding Your Motivations

Your motivations play a crucial role in your success when making money online. It is important to understand what drives you, whether it is financial freedom, the flexibility to work from anywhere, or the ability to pursue your passions. When you are clear about your motivations, it is easier to stay motivated and overcome obstacles when they arise.

Developing the Right Mindset

Making money online requires patience, persistence, and a willingness to learn and adapt. It is easy to get discouraged when things don't go as planned, but it's important to remember that success is not always immediate. The key is to keep moving forward, learning from your mistakes and keeping a positive attitude.

To develop the right mindset, focus on the following:

- Stay positive: Believe in yourself and your abilities, and don't let setbacks discourage you.
- Learn from your mistakes: Every failure is an opportunity to learn and improve.
- Stay motivated: Keep your goals and motivations in mind and remind yourself why you started.
- Surround yourself with positive influences: Look for mentors and join communities of like-minded individuals who will support and inspire you.

By setting your goals, understanding your motivations, and developing the right mindset, you will be well on your way to making money online. Remember, success takes time and effort, but with the right attitude and plan, you can achieve your financial goals and create the lifestyle you desire.

Understanding the Online Landscape: Opportunities and Challenges

———

Making money online is a broad and ever-changing field, with many opportunities and challenges to be aware of. In this chapter, we will discuss the different ways to make money online, the advantages and disadvantages of each, and the challenges you may face as you navigate the online landscape.

Ways to Make Money Online

There are many ways to make money online, including but not limited to:

- Freelancing: offering your skills to clients through platforms such as Upwork, Fiverr, and Freelancer.
- Online tutoring: providing one-on-one instruction through platforms such as Chegg and TutorMe.
- Selling products: leveraging online marketplaces such as Amazon, Etsy, and eBay.
- Online surveys: completing surveys for cash or gift card rewards through platforms such as Swagbucks and Survey Junkie.
- Affiliate marketing: promoting other people's products and earning a commission on each sale.
- Blogging: creating and monetizing a website through advertising, affiliate marketing, and sponsored posts.
- YouTube: creating and monetizing video content through advertising, sponsorships, and affiliate marketing.
- Social media: monetizing your followers through sponsored posts, brand deals, and affiliate marketing.

- Online courses: creating and selling educational content through platforms such as Udemy and Skillshare.
- E-commerce: starting and managing an online store.
- Cryptocurrency: investing and earning in the digital currency market.
- Real estate: using the internet to invest and earn money in the real estate market.

Advantages and Disadvantages of Each

Each method of making money online has its own advantages and disadvantages. For example, freelancing allows for flexibility and the ability to work from anywhere, but it also requires a significant amount of self-discipline and time management. Selling products online can be a great way to earn passive income, but it also requires a significant investment in inventory and marketing. Understanding the advantages and disadvantages of each method will help you determine which one is best suited for your skills and goals.

Challenges to Overcome

Making money online is not without its challenges. Some of the most common challenges include:

- Competition: the online landscape is highly competitive, and it can be difficult to stand out in a crowded market.
- Scams: there are many scams online, so it is important to be vigilant and do your research before investing your time and money.
- Self-discipline: working from home can be challenging, and it requires a high level of self-discipline to stay focused and motivated.
- Technical skills: many online earning methods require a certain level of technical skills, so it's important to be prepared to learn

and adapt as needed.

By understanding the online landscape, including the opportunities and challenges that come with it, you'll be well-prepared to navigate the online world and turn your online earning efforts into a sustainable income stream.

Freelancing: How to Monetize Your Skills

Freelancing is one of the most popular ways to make money online, allowing you to leverage your skills and expertise to earn money on your own terms. In this chapter, we will discuss the basics of freelancing, how to find and attract clients, and how to build a sustainable freelancing business.

The Basics of Freelancing

Freelancing is the act of providing services to clients on a project-by-project basis, rather than being employed by a company on a full-time basis. Freelancers can offer a wide range of services, including but not limited to:

- Writing and editing
- Graphic design
- Web development
- Programming
- Virtual assistance
- Consulting
- Translation
- Photography

To start freelancing, you'll need to identify your skills and expertise, create a portfolio of your work, and set up a platform to market your services and communicate with clients.

Finding and Attracting Clients

One of the biggest challenges of freelancing is finding and attracting clients. There are several ways to do this, including:

- Utilizing freelancing platforms: platforms such as Upwork, Fiverr, and Freelancer can connect you with potential clients looking for the services you offer.
- Networking: reaching out to your professional network, attending industry events and joining online communities can help you find clients.
- Building a website: creating a website can help you showcase your portfolio and services, making it easier for potential clients to find you.
- Marketing: leveraging social media and other marketing channels to promote your services can help you attract new clients.

Building a Sustainable Freelancing Business

Once you have clients, it's important to build a sustainable freelancing business by:

- Delivering high-quality work: providing excellent work will help you retain clients and attract new ones through word-of-mouth referral.

Communicating effectively: maintaining clear and open communication with clients will help ensure that projects are completed on time and to their satisfaction.

- Setting fair prices: charging fair prices that reflect the value of your work will help you attract clients and build a sustainable business.
- Continuously learning and improving: staying up-to-date with industry trends and continuing to develop your skills will help you stay competitive and attract new clients.
- Building a team: as your business grows, you may need to hire

additional freelancers or employees to help with certain tasks, such as accounting or marketing.

Managing Your Time and Finances

Managing your time and finances effectively is crucial for the success of your freelancing business. Some tips for managing your time and finances include:

- Setting clear goals: setting goals for your business will help you stay focused and motivated.
- Creating a schedule: setting a schedule for your work will help you stay on task and manage your time effectively.
- Tracking expenses: keeping track of your expenses will help you manage your finances and plan for growth.
- Invoicing and billing clients: invoicing and billing clients on time will help ensure that you get paid for your work.

In conclusion, freelancing is a great way to monetize your skills and earn money online. By understanding the basics of freelancing, finding and attracting clients, building a sustainable business, and managing your time and finances effectively, you can turn your freelancing efforts into a successful and profitable venture.

Online Tutoring: Turn Your Expertise into Income

———

Online tutoring is a great way to monetize your expertise and share your knowledge with others. In this chapter, we will discuss the basics of online tutoring, how to find and attract students, and how to build a successful and profitable tutoring business.

The Basics of Online Tutoring

Online tutoring is the act of providing one-on-one instruction to students over the internet. Tutors can offer a wide range of subjects and services, including but not limited to:

- Academic subjects such as math, science, and English
- Test preparation for standardized tests such as the SAT, ACT, and GRE
- Language instruction
- Music and art lessons
- Career coaching

To start online tutoring, you'll need to have a strong understanding of the subject you wish to teach, as well as the ability to communicate effectively with students. You'll also need to set up a platform for delivering your lessons, such as a video conferencing software or online classroom.

Finding and Attracting Students

One of the biggest challenges of online tutoring is finding and attracting students. There are several ways to do this, including:

- Utilizing online tutoring platforms: platforms such as Chegg and TutorMe can connect you with potential students looking for the services you offer.
- Networking: reaching out to your professional network and joining online communities can help you find students.
- Building a website: creating a website can help you showcase your expertise and services, making it easier for potential students to find you.
- Marketing: leveraging social media and other marketing channels to promote your services can help you attract new students.

Building a Successful and Profitable Tutoring Business

Once you have students, it's important to build a successful and profitable tutoring business by:

- Delivering high-quality instruction: providing excellent instruction will help you retain students and attract new ones through word-of-mouth referral.
- Communicating effectively: maintaining clear and open communication with students will help ensure that their learning needs are being met.

Setting fair prices: charging fair prices that reflect the value of your instruction will help you attract students and build a sustainable business.

- Continuously learning and improving: staying up-to-date with industry trends and continuing to develop your teaching skills will help you stay competitive and attract new students.
- Building a team: as your business grows, you may need to hire additional tutors or teaching assistants to help with certain

subjects or classes.

Managing Your Time and Finances

Managing your time and finances effectively is crucial for the success of your tutoring business. Some tips for managing your time and finances include:

- Setting clear goals: setting goals for your business will help you stay focused and motivated.
- Creating a schedule: setting a schedule for your classes and lesson preparation will help you stay on task and manage your time effectively.
- Tracking expenses: keeping track of your expenses will help you manage your finances and plan for growth.
- Billing students: billing students on time will help ensure that you get paid for your services.

In conclusion, online tutoring is a great way to monetize your expertise and earn money online. By understanding the basics of online tutoring, finding and attracting students, building a successful and profitable business, and managing your time and finances effectively, you can turn your tutoring efforts into a successful and profitable venture.

Selling Products: Leveraging Online Marketplaces

―――

S elling products online is a great way to monetize your skills, hobbies, and interests. In this chapter, we will discuss the basics of selling products online, how to find and leverage online marketplaces, and how to build a successful and profitable business.

The Basics of Selling Products Online

Selling products online is the act of offering goods for sale through an online platform. This can include physical products, digital products, or a combination of both. Some popular online marketplaces include Amazon, Etsy, and eBay. These marketplaces allow you to easily set up a store, list your products, and reach a large audience of potential customers.

To start selling products online, you'll need to identify a niche or product idea that you're passionate about, create a product or source a product, and set up an online store or listing on an online marketplace.

Finding and Leveraging Online Marketplaces

One of the biggest advantages of selling products online is the ability to reach a global audience. Online marketplaces provide a great way to do this by:

- Providing a built-in audience: marketplaces such as Amazon and Etsy already have a large customer base, making it easier for your products to be discovered.
- Offering easy-to-use tools: most marketplaces have simple and user-friendly tools for listing products, managing orders, and

tracking sales.

Handling logistics: marketplaces such as Amazon also handle the logistics of fulfillment and shipping, which can save you time and resources.

To find the right online marketplace for your products, consider factors such as the type of products you plan to sell, the target audience, and the fees and commissions associated with each marketplace. Once you have identified the right marketplace, it's important to optimize your listings and take advantage of any marketing or promotional opportunities offered by the marketplace.

Building a Successful and Profitable Business

Once you have set up your online store or marketplace listing, it's important to build a successful and profitable business by:

- Providing high-quality products: offering high-quality products at fair prices will help you attract and retain customers.
- Optimizing your listings: making sure your listings are accurate, detailed, and visually appealing will help increase visibility and sales.
- Building a brand: creating a strong brand identity will help you stand out in a crowded marketplace and attract loyal customers.
- Continuously learning and improving: staying up-to-date with industry trends and researching new products or niches will help you stay competitive and grow your business.

Managing Your Time and Finances

Managing your time and finances effectively is crucial for the success of your online business. Some tips for managing your time and finances include:

- Setting clear goals: setting goals for your business will help you stay focused and motivated.
- Creating a schedule: setting a schedule for your work will help you stay on task and manage your time effectively.
- Tracking expenses: keeping track of your expenses will help you manage your finances and plan for growth.
- Monitoring sales and profitability: monitoring your sales and profitability will help you make informed decisions about your business and identify areas for improvement.

In conclusion, selling products online is a great way to monetize your skills, hobbies, and interests. By understanding the basics of selling products online, finding and leveraging online marketplaces, building a successful and profitable business, and managing your time and finances effectively, you can turn your efforts into a successful and profitable venture. It's important to find the right marketplace that aligns with your product and target audience, optimize your listings and take advantage of any marketing opportunities, and continuously learn and improve to stay competitive. With the right mindset and strategies, you can turn your passion for creating and selling products into a successful online business.

Online Surveys: Making Money with Your Opinions

———

Online surveys are an easy and convenient way to make money online by providing your opinions and feedback on various topics. In this chapter, we will discuss the basics of online surveys, how to find and participate in surveys, and how to maximize your earning potential.

The Basics of Online Surveys

Online surveys are a form of market research in which individuals are asked to provide their opinions and feedback on a variety of topics, such as products, services, or advertising campaigns. Surveys can be conducted through various methods, including online questionnaires, phone interviews, and in-person focus groups.

Companies and organizations use the data collected from surveys to gain valuable insights into consumer preferences and behavior. In return for participating in surveys, individuals can earn cash, gift cards, or other rewards.

Finding and Participating in Surveys

There are many websites and apps that offer online surveys, such as Survey Junkie, Swagbucks, and Toluna. To find and participate in surveys, you can:

- Sign up for survey panel websites: these websites connect you with market research companies that conduct surveys.
- Check your email: many companies and organizations also conduct surveys via email.
- Use survey apps: there are also survey apps that you can

download to your phone and take surveys on-the-go.

When participating in surveys, it's important to:

- Read the instructions and eligibility requirements carefully
- Provide honest and accurate responses
- Complete the survey within the given time frame

Maximizing Your Earning Potential

To maximize your earning potential, it's important to:

- Sign up for multiple survey panel websites: this increases your chances of receiving more surveys.
- Complete your profile: many survey panel websites ask you to complete a profile, which allows them to match you with surveys that are relevant to your interests and demographics.
- Be consistent: regularly participating in surveys will increase your earning potential over time.

It's also important to keep in mind that online surveys are not a primary source of income, but rather a way to earn extra cash in your spare time.

In conclusion, online surveys are an easy and convenient way to make money online by providing your opinions and feedback. By understanding the basics of online surveys, finding and participating in surveys, and maximizing your earning potential, you can turn your spare time into extra cash. Just keep in mind that it will not be your primary source of income and be consistent with your participation.

Affiliate Marketing: How to Earn Commissions with Other People's Products

―――

A ffiliate marketing is a popular method of earning money online by promoting other people's products and earning a commission for each sale or lead generated. In this chapter, we will discuss the basics of affiliate marketing, how to find and join affiliate programs, and how to effectively promote affiliate products.

The Basics of Affiliate Marketing

Affiliate marketing is a performance-based marketing strategy in which an individual, known as an affiliate, promotes a product or service offered by a business or organization, known as the merchant. The affiliate earns a commission for each sale or lead generated as a result of their promotion.

Affiliate marketing can be done through various methods, including:

- Blogging: writing reviews, tutorials, and comparisons of products and including affiliate links.
- Social media: promoting affiliate products on social media platforms, such as Instagram and YouTube.
- Email marketing: promoting affiliate products through email campaigns.

Finding and Joining Affiliate Programs

There are many affiliate programs available across a variety of industries, such as Amazon Associates, Commission Junction, and ClickBank. To find and join affiliate programs, you can:

- Research industries and products that align with your interests and expertise.
- Look for "affiliate program" or "affiliate marketing" sections on company websites.
- Join affiliate networks, such as ShareASale and Rakuten Marketing, which connect affiliates with multiple merchants and affiliate programs.

Effectively Promoting Affiliate Products

To effectively promote affiliate products and earn commissions, it's important to:

Choose products that align with your interests and audience: promoting products that you are passionate about and that are relevant to your audience will increase the likelihood of conversions.

- Create high-quality content: whether it's a blog post, video, or social media post, make sure the content is well-researched, informative and engaging to increase the chances of people clicking on your affiliate links.
- Use a variety of promotion methods: don't limit yourself to just one method of promotion. Experiment with different methods such as email marketing, social media, and influencer marketing to reach a wider audience.
- Use tracking links: use unique tracking links for each promotion method to track your performance and optimize your efforts.
- Be transparent: disclose that you are using affiliate links and be

honest about your reviews and promotions, this will help to build trust with your audience.

- Stay up to date: Stay informed about new products, promotions, and industry trends. This will help you to stay relevant and capitalize on new opportunities.

In conclusion, affiliate marketing is a great way to earn money online by promoting other people's products and earning a commission for each sale or lead generated. By understanding the basics of affiliate marketing, finding and joining affiliate programs, and effectively promoting affiliate products, you can turn your passion and expertise into a profitable online business. Just keep in mind that you need to be consistent and use a variety of promotion methods, and stay informed about industry trends.

Blogging: Monetizing Your Website

Blogging has become a popular way to share information, express oneself and make money online. In this chapter, we will discuss the basics of blogging, how to create a successful blog and monetize it.

The Basics of Blogging

A blog is a type of website that features regular updates in the form of written articles, videos, or other types of content. Blogs can cover a wide range of topics, from personal experiences and thoughts, to news, and reviews. Blogging has become a popular way to share information, express oneself, and build an online presence.

Creating a Successful Blog

To create a successful blog, it's important to:

- Choose a niche: Pick a topic or niche that you are passionate about and that you can write about consistently.
- Choose a platform: Decide which platform you want to use to create your blog. Some popular choices include WordPress, Blogger, and Wix.
- Design and optimize your blog: Make sure your blog has a clean, professional design and that it is optimized for search engines.
- Create high-quality content: make sure your blog posts are well-researched, informative, and engaging to attract and retain readers.
- Promote your blog: Share your blog posts on social media, guest post on other blogs, and participate in online communities related to your niche to drive traffic to your blog.

Monetizing Your Blog

Once your blog has a sizable audience, you can start monetizing it through various methods, such as:

- Advertising: Place ads on your blog and earn money for each click or impression.
- Affiliate marketing: Include affiliate links in your blog posts and earn commissions for each sale or lead generated.
- Sponsored posts: Write sponsored posts or reviews for brands and earn money for each post.

Selling products or services: Use your blog as a platform to sell your own products or services, such as e-books, courses, or consulting services.

- Sponsorships: Partner with brands and businesses to offer sponsored content or collaborations.
- Email marketing: Build an email list and use it to promote products or services.
- Membership program: Create a membership program that offers exclusive content or perks for a monthly or annual fee.
- Crowdfunding: Use platforms like Patreon or Kickstarter to fund your blog and create exclusive content for backers.

In conclusion, blogging is a great way to share information, express oneself, and make money online. By choosing a niche, creating a successful blog, and monetizing it through various methods, you can turn your passion into a profitable online business. Remember to be consistent in creating high-quality content, promoting your blog and experimenting with different monetization methods to find the best fit for your blog.

YouTube: Creating and Monetizing Video Content

———

YouTube has become one of the most popular platforms for creating and sharing video content. In this chapter, we will discuss the basics of creating and monetizing video content on YouTube.

The Basics of Creating YouTube Videos

YouTube is a video-sharing platform where users can upload, share, and view videos. To create videos for YouTube, you will need:

- A camera or smartphone: to record your videos
- Video editing software: to edit and enhance your videos
- A YouTube account: to upload and share your videos

Once you have the necessary equipment and software, you can start creating videos. Some popular types of videos on YouTube include:

- Vlogs: personal diary-style videos that document your daily life and experiences
- How-to videos: tutorials and demonstrations on a specific topic or skill
- Product reviews: videos that review and evaluate products or services
- Comedy skits: videos that are meant to be funny and entertaining

Creating and Monetizing YouTube Videos

Once you have a YouTube channel with a sizable audience, you can start monetizing your videos through various methods, such as:

- Ad revenue: YouTube will place ads on your videos and pay you a portion of the ad revenue.
- Affiliate marketing: Include affiliate links in your videos and earn commissions for each sale or lead generated.
- Sponsored videos: Partner with brands and businesses to create sponsored videos.
- Selling products or services: Use your YouTube channel as a platform to sell your own products or services, such as e-books, courses, or consulting services.

YouTube Premium revenue: If your channel is part of YouTube's Partner Program, viewers can pay a monthly fee for an ad-free experience and access to exclusive content on your channel, and you will receive a portion of this revenue.

- Crowdfunding: Use platforms like Patreon or Kickstarter to fund your YouTube channel and create exclusive content for backers.
- Brand deals and collaborations: Partner with brands and businesses to create content and receive payment or products in return.

In conclusion, YouTube is a powerful platform for creating and sharing video content. By creating high-quality, engaging videos and building an audience, you can monetize your channel through various methods such as ad revenue, affiliate marketing, sponsored videos, and more. Remember to be consistent in creating and uploading videos and to experiment with different monetization methods to find the best fit for your channel. Additionally, be aware of the YouTube's guidelines and terms of service, as well as copyright laws, to avoid any issues.

Social Media: Making Money with Your Followers

———

S ocial media platforms have become one of the most popular ways to connect with people and share information. In this chapter, we will discuss the basics of making money with your followers on social media.

The Basics of Building a Social Media Presence

To build a social media presence, you need to:

- Choose a platform: Decide which platform(s) you want to use to build your presence. Some popular choices include Instagram, TikTok, Facebook, Twitter, and LinkedIn.
- Create a consistent and engaging brand: Develop a consistent aesthetic, tone and voice for your social media presence.
- Create high-quality content: Make sure your posts are well-researched, informative, and visually appealing to attract and retain followers.
- Promote your social media presence: Share your posts on other social media platforms, participate in online communities related to your niche, and use paid promotions to drive traffic to your social media accounts.

Monetizing Your Social Media Presence

Once you have a sizable following on social media, you can start monetizing your presence through various methods, such as:

- Sponsored posts: Write sponsored posts or reviews for brands and earn money for each post.

- Affiliate marketing: Include affiliate links in your posts and earn commissions for each sale or lead generated.
- Selling products or services: Use your social media presence as a platform to sell your own products or services, such as e-books, courses, or consulting services.
- Influencer marketing: Partner with brands and businesses to create sponsored content or collaborations.
- Brand deals and collaborations: Partner with brands and businesses to create content and receive payment or products in return.

In conclusion, social media is a powerful tool for building a personal brand, connecting with people, and making money online. By creating a consistent and engaging brand, creating high-quality content, and monetizing your social media presence through various methods, you can turn your online presence into a profitable business However, it's important to remember that building a significant following on social media takes time and effort, and success also relies on being consistent, engaging and honest with your audience. Also, it's important to disclose any sponsored or affiliated content on your social media platforms as it is a requirement by the Federal Trade Commission. Additionally, be aware of the terms and policies of the social media platform to avoid any issues.

Another important aspect to consider is to diversify your income streams, as relying on one source of revenue can be risky. Therefore, it is recommended to explore different monetization methods and find the ones that work best for you and your audience.

Overall, making money with social media is possible, but it requires strategic planning, hard work, and patience. By following the strategies outlined in this chapter, you can turn your social media presence into a profitable business.

Online Courses: Creating and Selling Educational Content

Online courses have become a popular way for individuals and businesses to share their knowledge and expertise with a global audience. In this chapter, we will discuss the basics of creating and selling online courses.

The Basics of Creating an Online Course

To create an online course, you need to:

- Choose a topic: Decide on a topic that you are knowledgeable and passionate about.
- Plan your course content: Organize your course content into manageable sections or modules.
- Create course materials: Use tools such as video recording software, screen recording software, or a learning management system to create the course materials.
- Promote your course: Use social media, email marketing, or paid advertising to promote your course to potential students.

Monetizing Your Online Course

Once your course is created, you can monetize it through various methods such as:

- Selling the course directly: Host and sell your course on your own website or through an online course platform such as Udemy or Coursera.
- Offering a subscription model: Offer access to your course on a

recurring basis, such as on a monthly or annual basis.

- Creating a membership site: Create a membership site where students have access to your course and other exclusive content.
- Consulting services: Offer consulting services to students who have completed your course.

In conclusion, creating and selling online courses is a great way to share your knowledge and expertise with a global audience, and to monetize your skills and expertise. However, it is important to keep in mind that creating a successful online course takes time, effort and planning. Additionally, it's important to be aware of the competition, to do research and to find out what is already available, so you can differentiate your course and make it stand out . Also, it's important to consider the target audience of your course and to tailor the content and marketing to their needs and interests. Additionally, it's important to ensure that your course is engaging and interactive, by using a variety of multimedia and interactive elements to keep the students interested and motivated.

Another important aspect to consider is the price of your course. It's important to find the right balance between making a profit and making your course accessible to as many students as possible. One way to do this is to offer a free preview of your course or to offer a money-back guarantee, so that potential students can try the course before committing to it.

In summary, creating and selling online courses is a great way to monetize your skills and expertise, but it requires time, effort, and planning. By following the strategies outlined in this chapter, you can successfully create and sell online courses, and share your knowledge with a global audience.

E-commerce: Starting and Managing an Online Store

E-commerce has become an increasingly popular way for individuals and businesses to sell products and services online. In this chapter, we will discuss the basics of starting and managing an online store.

Getting Started: Choosing a Platform and Registering Your Business

The first step to starting an online store is to choose an e-commerce platform such as Shopify, WooCommerce, or Magento. These platforms provide the necessary tools and functionality for setting up and managing an online store. Once you have chosen a platform, you'll need to register your business and obtain any necessary licenses and permits.

Setting Up Your Online Store

Once you have registered your business, you'll need to set up your online store by:

- Choosing a design template or creating a custom design
- Adding products and pricing information
- Setting up payment and shipping options
- Creating a checkout process
- Adding a privacy policy and terms of service

Promoting and Marketing Your Online Store

After setting up your online store, the next step is to promote and market it. This can be done through various methods such as:

- Social media marketing: Use social media platforms such as

Facebook, Instagram, and Twitter to promote your store and products.

- Search engine optimization: Optimize your website for search engines such as Google and Bing to increase visibility and drive traffic to your store.
- Email marketing: Use email marketing to promote your store and products to existing and potential customers.
- Paid advertising: Use paid advertising such as Google AdWords or Facebook Ads to drive traffic to your store.

Managing Your Online Store

Managing an online store involves tasks such as:

- Tracking and analyzing website traffic and sales data
- Fulfilling orders and managing inventory
- Providing customer service and support
- Keeping your website and products updated

In conclusion, starting and managing an online store can be a great way to monetize your products and services. However, it requires planning, effort and time. Additionally, it's important to keep in mind that e-commerce is a highly competitive market, so it's essential to differentiate your store and products, to stay ahead of the competition and to constantly analyze your data and improve your strategy. With the right approach, you can successfully start and manage an online store and achieve your financial goals.

Cryptocurrency: Investing and Earning in the Digital Currency Market

―――

Cryptocurrency has become an increasingly popular way for individuals and businesses to invest and earn money. In this chapter, we will discuss the basics of investing and earning in the digital currency market.

Understanding Cryptocurrency

Before investing or earning in cryptocurrency, it's important to understand what it is and how it works. Cryptocurrency is a digital or virtual currency that uses cryptography for security. It operates independently of a central bank or government and is decentralized, meaning it is not controlled by any single institution. Some of the most popular cryptocurrencies include Bitcoin, Ethereum, and Litecoin.

Investing in Cryptocurrency

Investing in cryptocurrency can be a high-risk, high-reward endeavor. To invest in cryptocurrency, you'll need to:

- Choose a cryptocurrency to invest in: Research different cryptocurrencies and their potential for growth.
- Choose a platform to invest on: Platforms such as Coinbase, Binance, and Kraken allow individuals to buy and sell cryptocurrencies.
- Buy the cryptocurrency: Use the platform to buy the cryptocurrency of your choice.

It's important to keep in mind that the value of cryptocurrency can be highly volatile, and past performance is not indicative of future results.

It's essential to do your research, understand the risks and to have a well-defined investment strategy.

Earning Cryptocurrency

There are several ways to earn cryptocurrency such as:

- Mining: Cryptocurrency mining is the process of solving complex mathematical problems to validate transactions and add new coins to the network. This process requires specialized computer hardware and software, and it can be expensive.

Trading: Cryptocurrency trading involves buying and selling cryptocurrencies on an exchange, similar to stock trading. This can be a high-risk, high-reward endeavor, and it requires knowledge of the market and a well-defined trading strategy.

- Staking: Some cryptocurrencies, such as Ethereum 2.0, allow individuals to "stake" their coins, which means they can earn a return on their investment by holding and validating transactions on the network.
- Affiliate marketing: Some companies in the cryptocurrency space offer affiliate programs, which allow individuals to earn commissions by promoting their products or services.
- Online surveys and microtasks: Some platforms pay users in cryptocurrency for completing online surveys or small tasks.
- Creating and selling your own cryptocurrency-related content or services: If you have knowledge or expertise in the cryptocurrency space, you can monetize it by creating and selling your own content or services.

In conclusion, the cryptocurrency market can be a great opportunity for individuals and businesses to invest and earn money. However, it is important to keep in mind that the market is highly volatile and uncertain, and the value of different cryptocurrencies can be highly unpredictable. It's essential to have a clear understanding of the risks, to do your research, to have a well-defined investment or earning strategy and to constantly monitor the market. With the right approach, you can successfully navigate the digital currency market and achieve your financial goals.

Investing in Real Estate: Using the Internet to Make Money

R eal estate investing has been a popular way to generate income for centuries, and the internet has made it easier than ever to get started. In this chapter, we will discuss the different ways you can use the internet to make money in the real estate market.

Online Real Estate Marketplaces

Online real estate marketplaces such as Zillow, Redfin, and Realtor.com make it easy to search for properties and connect with real estate agents. These platforms also allow investors to access property data, such as past sales prices and rental income, which can be helpful in making informed investment decisions. Some online real estate marketplaces also allow investors to purchase properties directly from the platform, eliminating the need to work with a real estate agent.

Real Estate Crowdfunding

Real estate crowdfunding platforms such as Fundrise and RealtyMogul allow investors to pool their money together to purchase properties. These platforms make it easy for individuals to invest in real estate, even if they don't have the cash to buy a property outright. Real estate crowdfunding also allows investors to diversify their portfolio by investing in multiple properties.

Online Property Management

The internet has also made it easier to manage properties remotely. Online property management platforms such as Cozy and Buildium allow landlords to handle tasks such as rent collection, maintenance requests, and tenant screening from their computer or smartphone. This can be a great option for investors who don't live near their properties or who don't have the time to manage them personally.

Online Real Estate Investment Groups

Online real estate investment groups such as BiggerPockets and the Real Estate Investors Association (REIA) provide a forum for investors to connect and share information. These groups can be a great resource for new investors, as they allow members to learn from more experienced investors and gain access to potential investment opportunities.

In conclusion, the internet has made it easier than ever to invest in real estate. By using online marketplaces, crowdfunding platforms, property management tools, and investment groups, investors can access a wealth of information and opportunities that were previously unavailable. With the right approach, you can use the internet to make money in the real estate market and achieve your financial goals.

Conclusion: Scaling Your Earnings and Staying Ahead of the Game

———

M aking money online is a great way to supplement your income or even replace your traditional job. However, it's important to remember that earning money online takes time, effort and patience. In this chapter, we will discuss strategies for scaling your earnings and staying ahead of the game.

Diversify Your Income Streams

One of the best ways to scale your earnings is to diversify your income streams. Instead of relying on one method to make money, it's a good idea to have multiple streams of income such as freelancing, affiliate marketing, blogging, and e-commerce. This way, if one stream dries up, you still have other sources of income to fall back on.

Automation and Outsourcing

Another way to scale your earnings is to automate and outsource tasks. For example, if you are selling products online, you can use automation tools to handle tasks such as inventory management and order fulfillment. Additionally, you can outsource tasks such as customer service and social media management to virtual assistants. This will free up your time and allow you to focus on more important tasks, such as growing your business.

Keep Learning and Adapting

The online landscape is constantly changing, and it's important to stay ahead of the game by keeping up with the latest trends and technologies. This means staying informed about new platforms and tools, and being willing to adapt and try new methods of making money online. By being open to new opportunities and being willing to learn, you can stay ahead of the curve and continue to scale your earnings.

In conclusion, making money online is a great way to achieve financial freedom and flexibility. By diversifying your income streams, automating and outsourcing tasks, and staying informed and adaptable, you can scale your earnings and achieve your financial goals. Remember that earning money online takes time, effort and patience, and as long as you stay persistent you will be able to achieve your goals.

Also by Jim Stephens

Kindle Publishing Made Easy: Autopilot Cash With Amazon Kindle!
Million-Dollar Secrets of the Amazon Associates: How They Make Money From the Biggest Online Shopping Mall
Self-Publishing Made Easy: The Easy Way to Self-publish Your Own Books!
Scam Busters: How to Avoid the Most Popular Scams of Today!
Affiliate Marketing and Blogging
The Quick and Easy Guide of Diamonds
Government Information
Hiking and Camping
Koi Pond
Law Information Guide
Motor Homes Research
Affiliate Marketing and Success Systems
Online Shopping
Outsourcing Ebooks and Software Jobs
Personal Loans
Private Jet Charters
Private Yacht Charters
Internet Marketer Alpha Dog
Networking and Social Dominance in the Twenty-First Century
Copywriting Best Kept Secrets: A Training Course for Writing Great Copy
Starting Your Home Business

Affiliate Marketing for Beginners: You Will Never Succeed Unless You Take The Opportunity

A Guide to Creating the Most Appropriate Budgets for You: Additional Cash in Your Pocket

Various Advantages of Membership Websites: With Membership Websites, Create a Passive Income

Affiliate Marketing Made Simple: Avoid Common Errors and Thrive in Successes

Article Marketing Made Simple: It Is Not Necessarily Difficult to Succeed

Blogging Made Simple: Blogging Can Be Lucrative

Advertising That Pays: Increase Your Traffic and Leads

The Complete Guide to Copywriting: Creating Words That Sell

Affiliate Marketing Made Simple

The Affiliate Marketer's Manual

Aquarium Maintenance Made Simple

Beginner's Guide to Online Video Marketing

Blogging Fundamentals: Blogging is the Next Big Thing

Techniques for Advanced Search Engine Optimization: On Autopilot, Increase Your Traffic and Profits!

Article Marketing Secrets

Beginner's Guide to Black Hat SEO

Super Guide to Snowmobiling: The Best Places to Have a Great Time

Forest Adventure With Friends: A Captivating Story With a Lot of Fun

How to Advertise Like a Pro

My Journey Through Life: A Personal Memoir

The Art of Crafting Short Stories: A Guide to Writing and Publishing

The Ultimate Guide to Making Money Online: Proven Strategies and Tips for Success

Battlefield of Honor: Bravery and Sacrifice Tested In Ultimate Battle

Echoes of the Past: Unveiling History's Secrets

Warrior's Code: The Unbreakable Ethics of a Warrior

AI-Powered Marketing: The Future of Digital Advertising

Beyond Words: How ChatGPT is Revolutionizing Communication
The Language of AI: Exploring the Power of ChatGPT
Talking to Machines: The Fascinating Story of ChatGPT and AI
Language Models
Uncovering the Unknown: Tales of Mysterious Discoveries
Shadow Squadron: Inside Covert Operations
The Last Stand: The Triumph of Bravery in Desperate Times
Valor in the Skies: Courage and Sacrifice in Aerial Warfare
Courage, Sacrifice, and Honor: Tales from the Frontline Heroes

About the Publisher

Accepting manuscripts in the most categories. We love to help people get their words available to the world.

Revival Waves of Glory focus is to provide more options to be published. We do traditional paperbacks, hardcovers, audio books and ebooks all over the world. A traditional royalty-based publisher that offers self-publishing options, Revival Waves provides a very author friendly and transparent publishing process, with President Bill Vincent involved in the full process of your book. Send us your manuscript and we will contact you as soon as possible.

Contact: Bill Vincent at rwgpublishing@yahoo.com